D1453196

# MORE THAN AN
# ARK ON ARARAT

# MORE THAN AN ARK ON ARARAT

*Spiritual lessons learned while searching for Noah's ark*

## JAMES B. IRWIN
### with MONTE UNGER

**BROADMAN PRESS**
Nashville, Tennessee

SCENE ON THE FRONT COVER: The campsite of the 1982 High Flight expedition to Mount Ararat; SCENE ON THE BACK PANEL: Snowy Ararat

Dewey Decimal Classification: 221.93
Subject Headings: BIBLE. O. T.—ANTIQUITIES //
MOUNT ARARAT

Printed in the United States of America

**Library of Congress Cataloging in Publication Data**

Irwin, James B. (James Benson)
    More than an ark on Ararat.

    1. Noah's ark.  2. Ararat, Mount (Turkey)  3. Irwin, James B. (James Benson)  I. Title.
BS1238.N6I78   1985    222'.11093    85-4157
ISBN 0-8054-5018-1

# DEDICATION

We dedicate this book to all the members of the 1982 High Flight expedition to Mount Ararat—and most of all to *Scotty Duncan,* one of the members, who died of cancer a few months after that expedition.

*Members:*
Richard Daniel Bass, Jr., Dallas, Texas
John Miller Bradley, Jr., Birmingham, Alabama
Michael Howard Carpenter, Columbus, Ohio
John Michael Christensen, Boulder, Colorado
Eryl Alert Cummings, Farmington, New Mexico
Douglas Warner Dean, Beverly Hills, California
Scotty Duncan, Colorado Springs, Colorado
Kathy Duncan, Colorado Springs, Colorado
Yucel Donmez, Chicago, Illinois
Robinson H. Gowdey, Dallas, Texas
James B. Irwin, Colorado Springs, Colorado
John McIntosh, Crestline, California
Robert Roland Stuplich, Almont, Colorado
Monte Charles Unger, Colorado Springs, Colorado

# Preface

I've been interested in Noah's ark since I was a young lad in Sunday School. The journey to the moon opened up new doors. I was speaking in Farmington, New Mexico, in 1976 and met Eyrl Cummings, who is regarded as the American expert on the ark. He has spent forty years of his life researching it and has been to Turkey's Mount Ararat seventeen times.

I thought it would be interesting to look for the ark, so I told Cummings that if he needed anyone to carry his bags or keep him company, I'd love to go with him. About a year later, he called me to go with him to Turkey. However, the primary purpose of that trip was to look for the Ark of the Covenant—we found a new cave on Mount Nebo in Jordan.

After our work in Jordan, we went into Eastern Turkey. Unfortunately, the groundwork had not been sufficient, and the Turkish government wouldn't allow us to go on Mount Ararat. I did see the prime minister and presented him with a Turkish flag I'd carried to the moon.

My interest continued to build. Cummings called me in 1982 and asked me to be the leader of an expedition to find the ark. I wrote to the Turkish president and told him of my desires. Very surprisingly, about a month later, I received a letter from him inviting me to come to Turkey and look for the ark as his guest. We accepted his invitation and searched on the north slope from the Kop plain east to the Ahora Gorge. This book is a result of that expedition.

JAMES B. IRWIN
Colorado Springs, Colorado

# Contents

# I.

# INTRODUCTION: MORE THAN AN ARK ON ARARAT!

Mount Ararat in Turkey, where the High Flight expeditions hope to find Noah's ark (Photo by John McIntosh)

# 1
# Upon the Mountains of Ararat

"And in the seventh month, on the seventeenth day of the month, the ark came to rest upon the mountains of Ararat. Then God said to Noah, 'Go forth from the ark, you and your wife, and your sons and your sons' wives with you'" (Gen. 8:4,15-16, RSV).

One of the most intriguing aspects of climbing Mount Ararat is that at any moment we might be walking where everyone's childhood hero, Noah, walked as he led his water-weary family down the mountain.

We were in the place where life began anew, so it was special being on this holy mountain.

The search for Noah's ark has been well-documented and chronicled in many books and articles. Therefore, this book, though it does use our expedition as the cohesive thread throughout, takes a new direction. It tells what we did discover on the mountain, even though we didn't discover the ark.

We found something far more important.

# 2
# The Discovery of the Unseen

It had started out so promising. We had finally received the hard-to-get-permission to climb the desolate mountain from Turkey's president, General Kenan Evren.

One of the reasons gaining permission is so difficult is because of the political and military sensitivity of Mount Ararat. It is tucked away in the easternmost prong of Turkey, only a few miles from Russia to the north and Iran to the east. Because of this strategic zone, three elite Turkish commandos, armed with machine guns, accompanied our entire expedition.

While we were on the north slopes, we could not only look down onto a Russian city, but we could hear Russian voices on our walkie-talkies. The day I was seriously injured in a fall, the Russians were on all our radio frequencies, making communications difficult, to say the least. But we felt that gaining the Turkish government's permission was the first good sign.

The group was optimistic to start with, but this optimism heightened during our first afternoon on the mountain. It began raining, quickly turning into a pelting hailstorm. The thunder boomed like loud artillery explosions all around us. When the hail stopped, the sun came out one more time before setting. Like weary animals emerging from warm burrows, we all crawled out of our tents and saw a rainbow right over our camp.

This wasn't a rainbow off in the distance. At first, some

of the men didn't see it because they were looking toward the horizon. It arched right over us! What more Noah-like sign did we need? There was something particularly eerie about seeing a rainbow right where the first rainbow had been seen. We felt we had been blessed—surely we would find the ark!

We had everything going for us: government permission, the benefit of all previous ark-hunting research, eager climbers, good weather (that rain/hailstorm was the only bad weather we had), the sign of the rainbow, and because I had been part of the Apollo mission which discovered the "Genesis" rock on the moon, I truly felt that God would allow me to find something even more significant from the Book of Genesis on the earth.

But we didn't find a shred of evidence of the ark, not a trace. So what was the trip all about? Surely God had *something* in mind for fourteen of His dedicated children who had invested time, energy, and money in this adventure.

For me, one of the great truths of the trip can be summed up in this verse, "So we fix our eyes not on what is seen, but on what is unseen. For what is seen is temporal, but what is unseen is eternal" (2 Cor. 4:18).

The ark was the objective, but there were many "unseen" things going on in our lives. For the Christian, much of life is like this. We live in a different kingdom; we have values not seen or understood by the world's system; we live by faith, which is unseen; and it is these unseen things that truly matter, because they are eternal.

Actually, we can learn this lesson from Noah himself, for Hebrews 11:1-2,7 says, "Now faith is being . . . . certain of what we do not see. This is what the ancients were commended for. By faith Noah, when warned about things not yet seen, in holy fear built an ark to save his family."

This book is for everyone who has ever taken an outdoor adventure and for those who enjoy armchair adventures; but, most of all, it is for all who are interested in the inward spiritual journey, which is the most splendid adventure of all.

# 3
# More Than an Ark on Ararat

It is obvious that man's objectives aren't always God's objectives, but we do tend to lose sight of this when we are in the pursuit of an important goal.

If we focus exclusively on reaching a goal (whether it be finding a mate, making money, reaching an executive position, developing a significant ministry, or trying to discover Noah's ark), we may pass up *much of the other living* which occurs in the meantime.

Does it mean the trip was wasted when we didn't locate the ark? No, not for the Christian believer.

Proverbs 16:9 says, "In his heart a man plans his course, but the Lord determines his steps." Man is primarily interested in the final objective; but God has a different value system: since He is aware of each "sparrow" that falls and knows of "the very hairs of your head," so is He aware of and interested in *each of our steps.*

Because God is interested in every tiny detail of what we do while in the process of major goal achievement, what happens during a Christian's seemingly "idle" or "trivial" moments is highly pivotal to Him. Often these moments are more important *eternally* than world headlines, for these comprise the personal growth factors of the human spirit attempting to grow into Christlikeness.

That is why there was more than an ark on Ararat!

# II.

# IN TURKEY: THE ADVENTURE BEFORE THE ADVENTURE

# 4
# Terrorist Attack!

When we landed at Ankara's Esenboga Airport at 3:25 PM aboard a Lufthansa flight from West Germany, we were surprised to see soldiers everywhere, even on the runway. Because we'd been traveling day and night, we didn't know that there had been a terrorist attack on the airport the previous afternoon.

There had been a two-hour long gunfight. The terrorists attacked with submachine guns and explosives. In cold blood, they brazenly strafed innocent passengers going through passport control: six were killed, and seventy-two were wounded.

We saw the bullet holes in the walls, ceiling, and windows. Many areas were still roped off by the military.

Authorities thought the terrorists had arrived on our same Lufthansa flight the day before. This means if we would have come a day earlier, we would have arrived *with* the terrorists and perhaps would have become their victims!

Psalm 140:1-2 says:

> Rescue me, O Lord, from evil men;
>    protect me from men of violence,
> who devise evil plans in their hearts
>    and stir up war every day.

We truly felt protected by our Heavenly Father.

Turkish soldiers pulling guard duty outside of the expedition's motel
(Photo by John Bradley, Jr.)

# 5
# Our Turkish Motel Was Like a Military Garrison

After seeing the bullet-splattered walls at the Ankara airport and hearing about the possibility of terrorist attacks in eastern Turkey, where we were headed, it gave us peace of mind to be continually guarded by the tough Turkish soldiers.

The Sim-er Motel, the staging area of most Ararat expeditions, is on a barren stretch of highway a few miles east of the small, sleepy town of Dogubeyazit and sixteen miles west of the Iranian border. But the desolate location on the high Anatolian plateau has one redeeming factor—it gives an unrestricted view of Mount Ararat.

We arrived at the Sim-er late at night. The motel was like an armed camp. There were guards, some armed with rifles and others with machine guns, in the front, back, and on all sides. They were in the hallways, by all exits, and at every corridor corner. When we left our rooms to go to the dining room or to visit a friend, we always encountered a soldier. We felt safe and secure.

It was much like Paul's words to the struggling, fearful Christians in Philippi, "Have no anxiety about anything, but in everything by prayer and supplication with thanksgiving let your requests be made known to God. And the peace of God, which passes all understanding, will *keep* your hearts and your minds in Christ Jesus" (Phil. 4:6-7, RSV).

The word "keep" in the Greek is a military term meaning "shall keep guard over." Philippi was a Roman garrison town, and the inhabitants were accustomed to seeing Roman soldiers on guard duty.

As we saw the Turkish soldiers keeping guard over us, it gave great peace, just as praying about our needs and anxieties gives us the peace of God which will guard over our "hearts" (emotions) and "minds" (thoughts).

# 6
# Commandos Don't Get Cold!

It was chilly on Turkey's high plateau at dawn. A biting wind cut into several of us as we were jogging the day before the Ararat ascent. The skies were clear, except over Ararat which, like the modest Moslem women who veil their faces, still wouldn't reveal its magnificence to us.

We were dressed warmly in our jogging suits, but the Turkish commando officer who accompanied us wore combat boots, fatigue pants, a pistol strapped to his hip, and was bare from the waist up.

We had been jogging awhile, the cold stinging our faces. I asked the officer, "Aren't you cold?"

He replied, "I'm a commando, sir. Commandos don't get cold!"

This rugged officer has given his life to soldiering. He received training with the U.S. Army Rangers, Pathfinders, Paratroopers, and with the British Commandos. He is now an instructor at the Turkish Commando School. Any ordinary Turkish soldier is tough, let alone one who leads other commandos.

He not only expected hardness, but sought the harder way to toughen him up even more. The night before reaching our staging area, we were all crammed into a military bus, which stirred up dust from the rough gravel road. Some were complaining. The commando commented, "This dust is good training."

Everything in his life pertained to his ultimate goal of

being a good Turkish commando. Sure, the dust bothered him, sure he was cold, but he endured the hardness.

Second Timothy 2:3-4 says, "Endure hardship with us like a good soldier of Christ Jesus. No one serving as a soldier gets involved in civilian affairs—he wants to please his commanding officer."

Do we, as Christians, take the easy way out too often? Or do we endure the rigors of the spiritual battle, being a good soldier for Christ and living to please Him, our Commanding Officer?

# 7
# We Found Provisions, But Would We Find the Ark?

After our morning jog and a Turkish breakfast of yogurt, olives, bread, jam, and extremely strong coffee, we set off for the Dogubeyazit marketplace to see if we could get fresh food to supplement our dried camping food.

Several soldiers accompanied us to the small village. We were amazed to see the richness and variety of fresh fruits and vegetables. Shelves were filled with grains, pickles, cheeses, olives, nuts, bread, peaches, grapes, tomatoes, lemons, watermelons, onions, eggplant, potatoes, and peppers. It looked like the horn of plenty in this dry, dusty little village!

We thought of Psalm 23:1, "The Lord is my shepherd, I shall lack nothing" and Psalm 34:10, "Those who seek the Lord lack no good thing." We would have fresh food on Ararat to nourish us when we returned from the daily treks into the wilderness.

We did the bulk of our shopping at one of the dozens of stalls in the marketplace. As we bought from this one shopkeeper, he beamed, for it was to be his day of good fortune. But three doors away, another shopkeeper watched us sadly. As we piled up more and more supplies, his sadness turned to anger. He was probably thinking, "Why didn't they come to my shop?" A youth entered his stall, pointed to us, and said something. The angry shopkeeper slapped him on the side of the head, then stalked to the back of the shop where he couldn't see all of his profits draining away.

Jim Irwin accompanied by Turkish soldiers to the marketplace in Dogubeyazit (Photo by Bob Stuplich)

Psalm 75:6-7 says,

No one from the east or the west or from the desert
    can exalt a man.
But it is God who judges:
He brings one down, he exalts another.

Would we discover the ark and be like the shopkeeper who had good fortune this day? Or would we be like the other shopkeeper? Would we come away empty-handed? And if we did find nothing, what would be our attitude?

# 8
# Eating Bread in a Turkish Army Truck

It was finally time to begin our ascent of the mountain.

We had gone to bed at midnight and were awakened at 2:30 AM. We had only two and a half hours of rest to prepare us for a full day's climb to our 11,500-foot base camp on the broad meadow near Lake Kop, where we finally arrived in the late afternoon.

But at this early morning hour we were in the back of an open army truck as it rumbled over the rough gravel roads. We were jerked and slammed against the sides. We had no blankets, so we huddled together for warmth.

Though it was still pitch dark, we could see the white top of the mountain. Its enormity was magnificent and awesome. We'd look away for a moment, only to look back again, our gaze irrevocably drawn to the mysterious Ararat. Venus shone brightly between Noah's mountain and Little Ararat, a smaller, cone-shaped mountain just to the east.

It was an exciting beginning to our adventure. And to add to the drama, just as we left Dogubeyazit, where we had stopped to get several dozen loaves of freshly baked bread, the Muslim call to prayer was played over the mosque's loudspeakers. The long, wailing notes sailed across the city, awakening the faithful to begin their morning prayers. It was 4:30 AM.

We hadn't eaten breakfast, so we broke open some of the two-foot-long loaves. The hard crust had kept the heat inside, like the jacket of a baked potato does. The warmth hitting the cold air made the bread steam, as if it were alive, breathing. So as the Muslims were prostrate before their Allah, we were reminded by this "breathing" bread that we were in the presence of our living Christ, who said, "I am the bread of life. He who comes to me will never go hungry." (John 6:35).

We ate those Turkish loaves for over a week, and kept hungering for more; at the same time, we ate from the Word of God, which satisfied completely. "Man does not live on bread alone, but on every word that comes from the mouth of God" (Matt. 4:4).

# III.

# ON ARARAT: THE MOUNTAIN OF NOAH

Barren, treeless Ararat on a foggy day (Photo by Monte Unger)

# 9
# A Mountain Without Trees

There is a strangeness about Ararat.

You don't notice it at first, because of the novelty of just being there and because you are looking for the prow of the ark behind every rock.

But *then* you notice it: there are no trees. No "whispering in the pines," no "rustle of the leaves." The entire immensity of Ararat is absolutely devoid of even a single tree.

It is as if a mob of mythical giants of old used the mountain as their personal battleground, uprooting trees and flailing each other with them, until, over the weary centuries, there were no trees left, and the brooding giants stalked away from the devastation in search of another paradise in which to do battle.

Today, as birds fly over the mountain, dropping seeds already swallowed, and as the wind carries other tree seeds to the plateaus of Ararat, attempting to start a new forest, the soil screams, "No!" Too tired to give birth, like a worn and ravaged womb, the wounded soil says, "No more trees. I have suffered too many deaths. All my children have been taken from me. I can bear no more."

So Ararat is desolate, a mountain without trees.

It reminds one of Sarah in Genesis 11:30, who was ". . . barren; she had no children." We saw the mountain that way. But in Genesis 21:1-2, it says, "Now the Lord was gracious to Sarah. . . . [she] became pregnant and bore a son to Abraham in his old age." Would this be the trip where the ark would be revealed once again to man?

# 10
# The Map That Didn't Work

We were given a map made by a man who declared he saw the ark some years ago. We obeyed his instructions, "Follow the sheep trail up from Lake Kop until you reach . . ."

We followed that trail, but either the instructions were wrong or later generations of sheep had blazed new trails, for there were many narrow paths twisting in and out of the rocks.

It was like a weird dream in which you are given simple instructions on how to reach somewhere, but when you begin following those instructions, they turn into a nightmarish maze.

So it was with the man's words which attempted to guide us. They didn't work anymore, like an archaic language spoken in a new age. We, the new citizens, couldn't make any sense of it.

As Christians, we have been given another map, one for our spiritual direction in life. It is the Bible. Second Timothy 3:16-17 says, "All Scripture is God-breathed and is useful for teaching, rebuking, correcting and training in righteousness, so that the man of God may be thoroughly equipped for every good work."

But with this map, we are not left alone, as we were with the man's map on Mount Ararat. Jesus told us in John 14:26, "But the Counselor, the Holy Spirit, whom the Father will send in my name, will teach you all things and will remind you of everything I have said to you." The Counselor (or Comforter) is with us daily, guiding us; but the man with the map left us alone on the mountain.

# 11
# The People Who Climb Ararat

People climb Mount Ararat for three basic reasons: the locals climb it to shepherd their sheep on the high plateaus; others are simply mountain climbers; and many foreigners climb it trying to find the remnants of Noah's ark.

The shepherds have had far more luck than the others. Weather has turned back many mountaineers. And throughout the history of mankind, there has been *no positive proof* of any rediscovery of the ark, though there have been countless "sightings."

The reason for our expedition was to bring back scientific proof of the existence of the ark.

We found none.

"Many are the plans in a man's heart, but it is the Lord's purpose that prevails" (Prov. 19:21).

# 12
# God Desires Love More Than Grand Schemes

Once, early in the expedition, one man was washing the communal cookware after the evening meal. This was his job, but some of the climbers put their personal dishes in with the communal pots and pans, expecting him to wash those as well.

The dishwasher balked. This had happened several times already, and wasn't part of the bargain.

He went to a friend in the group, explained the situation, "They are taking advantage of me. I'm not going to wash their personal dishes. What do you think I should do?" He was angry and on the verge of becoming bitter.

The friend saw what was happening. It was still early in the trip. It was a critical moment for the dishwasher—one that could make him bitter and defensive for the remainder of the expedition, an attitude which could poison the camp atmosphere.

The friend answered, "That's right. They are taking advantage of you. I guess this is what Jesus was talking about when He said, 'If someone forces you to go one mile, go with him two miles'" (Matt. 5:41).

The dishwasher looked at him, still not quite convinced. That was a good Bible verse, but he was up to his elbows in dirty dishwater. The others were lounging around camp. He glared at them.

Then the friend rolled up his sleeves and suggested, "Even though they are asking you to do more than your fair share, this is precisely where Christianity is lived. If it doesn't work here, right now in this tough situation, then it isn't worth much. Let's put it to the test. I'll help you get all these dishes done."

The two of them washed up everything in sight. The dishwasher saw Christ's words being put into action by his friend. For the rest of the time on the mountain, the dishwasher went the extra mile every day, and his presence was scented with the fragrance of Christ.

The camp was at peace.

God is more concerned that we love one another than He is in our accomplishing some grand scheme. This is the entire message of 1 Corinthians 13. If we could paraphrase the key thought of that passage as it relates to our expedition, it would read, "If I find Noah's ark, and have not love, I am nothing."

# 13
# Maybe They Are Robbers

There is a bit of ancient doggerel about this mountain which goes,

"Such a traveller told you his last news,
  He saw the Ark a-top of Ararat;
  But did not climb there since 'twas getting late,
  And robber bands infest the mountain's foot.

We knew there was only a slight possibility of meeting up with robbers. A terrorist attack was a far greater possibility, which is the reason the commandos accompanied us.

One day two of us were crossing the broad plateau going toward the towering north canyon area, not too far from where I would have my near disastrous fall a few days later. We didn't have a soldier escort.

We saw a shepherd and some sheep on the other side of the plateau, just dots they were so far away. They were near the edge, where the plateau drops off into the clouds. It was pastoral, serene. We were alone, high above the turmoil of life below.

But then, much closer, we saw movement from behind some large rocks. Two men were walking briskly toward us, much faster than the shepherd's casual stroll. These men had something else on their minds. They were waving their hands and yelling. We weren't sure if they were motioning for us to get off the plateau or if they wanted us to stop. We weren't sure if they were Russian spies, robbers, terrorists, or what.

What to do?

We thought about moving higher up the canyon wall and going back to our base camp through a deep cleavage in the mountains near Parrot Glacier. But that was a long, hard climb. And maybe they could outclimb us! None of the other expedition members were nearby, so we couldn't shout for help. We had no weapons. And we couldn't get back to the camp from the way we had come, for the strangers had that blocked off.

As they got closer, we saw that they were tough. Square, rugged chins. A rough stubble of beard. They weren't smiling. They were yelling in another language.

We were still new to the mountain, this being only the first day of exploration. We were unsure of ourselves. The two men were closing in on us, still moving swiftly, looking like professional bouncers about to put us off the mountain.

We debated. Should we move on and get away from the ruffians? "No, let's greet them." We smiled and waved.

The strangers hesitated. Then they waved back and gave us gaped-tooth smiles. We reached out and shook hands.

They were friendly Turks, who just wanted to talk to us. We knew not one word of Turkish; they knew no English, yet we "talked" for half an hour. We took photographs; they gave us their addresses and wrote something else on the paper. When it was translated back at the camp, we learned they wanted us to get them jobs in America.

We could have been fearful and run away, or rude and ignored them. Instead we tried Proverbs 18:24, "A man that hath friends must shew himself friendly" (KJV).

# 14
# Who Were the Real Invaders?

The sheep invaded *our* camp!

They had been lurking on the fringes for several days, and finally made their move. They boldly marched right into and through our campsite, munching the grass between our tents, indiscriminately dropping their foul wastes, bleating, and making a general nuisance of themselves.

Our lovely, quiet meadow was desecrated. What right did they have?

But the deeper question was: Who was on whose turf? Were the sheep really the invaders? Or were we?

Think about it: the shepherd, with his mountain-sharp eyes, had seen us coming a few days earlier. He saw the thirty horses and mules carrying our packs and provisions, our mini-homes away from home. He saw us move a mountain of food up his mountain, so scarce of food.

He saw this caravan and wondered, *Where will those foreigners camp? Surely not on my sheep's best grazing ground on the lush meadow near Lake Kop? Surely not by the meadow's cool stream which provides the small pools of still water where sheep like to drink?*

Yes, we plunked right down on the sheep's dinner table. The grass where generations of sheep had been eating now lay flattened beneath our tents. The stream which had been the sheep's drinking fountain for centuries now cooled our drinks and watermelons.

Conquerors always come in and take.

Caught in the act—"raiders" and invaders of our campsite (Photo by Bob Stuplich)

Would we take?

No!

We were committed to leaving our campsite with no evidence we had been there. The shepherds would return again; we might never return.

We were visitors to Turkey. We were obligated to treat their hospitality with respect and, when we departed, to leave the dignity of Noah's holy mountain intact.

If the Turks were to camp on the hills behind my home, I'd want them to leave it clean. We could do no less. Jesus said, "Do to others as you would have them do to you" (Luke 6:31).

# 15
# What We Risked to Find the Ark

We were a band of committed Christians who had sacrificed money, time, and effort in trying to find the greatest archeological treasure of all history, the ark of Noah.

We faced risk of physical danger, for Ararat is a crumbling mountain. Every few minutes we could hear rockslides and small avalanches. A falling rock would knock me unconscious near the end of the expedition.

There were vicious sheep dogs, wolves, and bears. There was danger of attack by robbers and terrorists.

The quick-changing weather of Ararat has forced many explorers off the mountain when a warm, sunny day suddenly turned into an Arctic-type blizzard.

We slept in numbing cold, fell on loose rock, dodged tumbling boulders, grew exhausted from high-altitude climbing, had feet sore with blisters, had painfully cracked lips from sunburn, received various cuts and nicks, all in pursuit of a hidden and *uncertain* treasure. Even knowing the risks, no doubt many of you readers would have joined us on this adventure if you had been given the opportunity.

But I wonder if we Christians are as committed to finding an even greater treasure, one we are *certain* of finding, without all the risks and dangers. This is a hidden treasure we can seek in the comfort of our homes.

Proverbs 2:1-5 says,

> My son, if you accept my words
> and store up my commands within you,

turning your ear to wisdom
and applying your heart to understanding,
and if you call out for insight
and cry aloud for understanding,
and if you look for it as for silver
and search for it as for hidden treasure,
then you will understand the fear of the Lord
and find the knowledge of God.

This treasure of wisdom and understanding is hidden in the Scriptures, waiting for us to seek and find. Psalm 19:10 says that it is "more precious than gold,/than much pure gold . . . sweeter than honey,/than honey from the comb."

Bible study does take work. In fact, Proverbs says we should use the same effort in studying the Scriptures as if we were searching for hidden treasures. We risked much searching for the uncertain treasure of the ark; will we use the same effort looking for biblical treasures?

Acts 17:11 says, "These were more noble than those in Thessalonica, in that they received the word with all readiness of mind, and *searched* the scriptures daily, whether those things were so" (KJV, author's italics).

The next time we read about an exciting adventure or see a documentary of some grandiose search, we can remember the obtainable "treasures" awaiting us in the Scriptures.

The cool stream which flowed through the High Flight expedition's camp (Photo by John McIntosh)

# 16
# The Fear of Going Thirsty

Near our camp a narrow, but steady stream came down from the rocks above. Pure, cold water. It was flowing full all day—at the beginning of the expedition. But as the nights grew colder and the water froze more solid, it took longer and longer for the sun to melt the stream's source the next day.

One day it didn't run all morning. It began running later each day, until one day there was just a trickle in the late afternoon. The next day there was no water at all.

How do you keep an entire expedition stocked with water for cooking, washing, and drinking? Alarm!

We sent our porters higher into the mountains to bring back fresh water. But it was suspect, for we didn't know where it had come from. The purity was gone, and we had to boil it. It became more difficult for them to find water. The lack of water could terminate our expedition prematurely.

But in Christ, we have no such predicament. He promises in John 4:13-14, "Everyone who drinks this water will be thirsty again, but whoever drinks the water I give him will never thirst. Indeed, the water I give him will become in him a spring of water welling up to eternal life." In John 6:35, Jesus says, "He who believes in me will never be thirsty."

The thirst He quenches is the spiritual thirst of every person. Christ not only quenches this thirst, but does so for eternity!

Several expedition members walking on the "bowling-ball"-type rocks
(Photo by Monte Unger)

# 17
# It Isn't Easy to Walk on Ararat

In my previous book *(More Than Earthlings,* Broadman, 1983) in which I parallel my space experiences with Christian living, one of the chapter titles is "It Isn't Easy to Walk on the Moon."

For different reasons, it's also hard to walk on Ararat. It was particularly difficult to walk the north slope from Lake Kop to the Ahora Gorge. Ararat is an extinct volcano, and the north slope consists almost entirely of loose tailings of lava rock, which makes it much like walking on stacked bowling balls.

We slipped and fell innumerable times. Our ice axes, serving as canes, kept us from falling even more. Our thick climbing boots protected our toes and ankles.

There was no solid footing. Some rocks would roll away beneath us, starting small landslides. For hours almost every step would be on rocks that moved. This created extreme discomfort. Each step had to be calculated. You prepared yourself to slide, twist, and slip. Not only was it physically exhausting, the uncertainty of it all was mentally fatiguing.

It was such a relief to reach some of the larger, solid rocks and walk even a few yards with certainty. That gave us ease and comfort.

We have that kind of certainty when we walk with God. He is solid rock and is The Solid Rock. Deuteronomy 32:4 affirms,

He is the Rock, his works are perfect,
and all his ways are just.
A faithful God who does no wrong,
upright and just is he.

When we turn over our lives to Him and truly decide to walk with Him, He says, "'For I know the plans I have for you,' declares the Lord, 'plans to prosper you and not to harm you, plans to give you hope and a future'" (Jer. 29:11).

When we walked on Ararat, we felt that harm could come to us at any time. When we walk with God we can be certain that His plans are not going to harm us.

# 18
# The Night the Tent Burned

It was bitterly cold on Ararat at night; water even froze in our tents. Our man-and-wife-cook team burned a candle in their tent one night for extra warmth. They fell asleep with the candle still burning.

In the middle of the night one of the soldiers awakened and saw flickering flames. At first he thought it was the fire of an early-morning hiking party, but realized it was far too early for that. He rushed out of his tent.

Seeing the couple's tent on fire, he smothered the flames with his raincoat. He shouted for them to clear out of the burning tent. They escaped with no injuries; the commando had slight burns on his hands; and the tent had a large hole that needed repair the next day.

Proverbs 6:27 asks, "Can a man scoop fire into his lap/without his clothes being burned?" In context, this verse speaks of a specific sin, but I think it can also warn us of any temptation. If any weakness is too tempting, we should not even entertain thoughts about it, for, as the candle in the tent, it could be potentially hazardous.

# 19
# Beware When the Going Gets Too Easy!

We had finally crossed the bowling ball-type rocks and were on solid earth again, quite near the Ahora Gorge. It was smooth, grassy terrain with short-tufted, high tundra grass. It was easy to walk.

One of the commandos, who couldn't speak English, pointed to the earth, gave a look of relief, and stamped his foot to show how easy it would be to walk now.

We all relaxed and began walking across the easy part. The Turk took a couple of steps, and the toe of his thick boot hit an inch-high rock sticking up through the grass. He stumbled and almost fell.

We all laughed. He laughed, too, and rolled his eyes skyward, as if to comment, "How foolish of me."

Aren't we like that in the Christian life?

We have handled a trying passage of living well because we gave it considerable care and took counsel with God at every turn. But when life becomes easier, we depend upon our own balance. We think *we* can do it without diligent attention to the Word of God to continually guide us.

First Corinthians 10:12 puts it like this: "So, if you think you are standing firm, be careful that you don't fall!" The secret is not to trust in self, but in Him. Proverbs 3:5-6 challenges:

Trust in the Lord with all your heart
and lean not on your own understanding;
in all your ways acknowledge him, and he will make
    your paths straight.

# 20
# Not All Is as It Seems

We sat high on one of the north slope canyons looking down onto undulating green hills, to the grays and browns. We could usually trace the path of the lava where it had flowed down the sides in earlier eruptions. The twisted, torturous, gnarled crust was now at rest, bulging up through green meadows where sheep grazed peacefully.

It was a peaceful view. White clouds dotted the horizon above Russia. Other snow-capped peaks towered up from the Soviet plains. Somewhere down there in those rolling hills was the Soviet-Turkish border. All seemed tranquil. But such a view is deceptive.

We learned that while we were walking the upper slopes of the mountain, there had been a border skirmish, during which the Soviet border guards had shot and killed two Turks.

As Jesus explained when he sent us out into the world, "I am sending you out like sheep among wolves. Therefore be as shrewd as snakes and as innocent as doves. But be on your guard against men" (Matt. 10:16-17). We must realize that while we are in the midst of a more tranquil pursuit, the "real world" is still there. We must be shrewd as snakes when we view a scene that appears innocent; chances are there are wolves lurking nearby.

One expedition member backpacking across an easy plateau (Photo by Monte Unger)

# 21
# The Hiker Has Two Backpacks

We each took two backpacks to Ararat: a larger one which contained all of our gear, and a smaller one which was for one-day forages. To travel light, we would carry only the essentials for one day in the wilderness, with emergency items (in case we were caught in a blizzard) in the smaller pack.

As Christians we have a similar equivalent. We have a larger, complete pack—the entire Bible which is our guide through life. We also can have a small "day" pack by carrying a small Testament wherever we go—for meditating in spare moments, for personal evangelism, and for help with spiritual problems.

The psalmist testified: "I will never forget your precepts,/for by them you have renewed my life" (Ps. 119:93).

# 22
# A Representative of the President

One day our commando officer went down to the village of Ahora with one of our climbers. They were seeking information from anyone who knew the whereabouts of Noah's ark. As you know, stories abound concerning people who say they know where the ark is. We wanted to put this to the test.

The commando told the people that he was a representative of the president of Turkey and that "these people" (meaning our expedition members) were guests of the president. Therefore, he was acting as an ambassador for the Turkish president and was able to intercede for us with the villagers.

As Christians, we are also ambassadors. Second Corinthians 5:20 says, "We are therefore Christ's ambassadors, as though God were making his appeal through us. We implore you on Christ's behalf: Be reconciled to God."

Our greatest mission on earth is the Great Commission, "Go into all the world and preach the good news to all creation" (Mark 16:15).

The good news is that Christ died for the sins of the world, and that anyone who confesses his sins and embraces Christ as personal Lord and Savior will receive forgiveness and have eternal life.

# IV.

# THE FALL: ASTRONAUT DOWN!

Jim was in rough condition when he was found after his near-fatal fall
(Photo by Monte Unger).

# 23
# Rockslide

I was traveling alone, disregarding the instructions I'd given everyone else.

One morning I had hoped to reach the summit with a small group of climbers, but I was moving too slowly. Disappointed with my performance and wanting to conserve my strength, I left the group. I headed back down to base camp in order to coordinate our move off the mountain, which had been planned for the next day.

I set out for the rocky ridge down Ark Rock, but around noon saw a shortcut down a snowfield.

It was slippery, so I sat down to put on my crampons, and that's the last thing I remember until near dusk. I must have been struck from behind by a falling rock.

The next thing I knew I was at the bottom of the snowfield in a pile of sharp rocks, and I was a bloody mess. I had broken five teeth, had several jagged gashes on the top of my head, a deep cut over my right eye and on the bridge of my nose, a sprained neck, a badly sprained ankle, sore ribs, and numerous other cuts and gashes on my face, hands, and legs.

I tried to stand, but was so weak from the loss of blood that my legs simply wouldn't support me. Fortunately, I had my sleeping bag in my backpack, which was miraculously still on my back. It was almost dark at this point. I was shivering in the cold. I climbed into my sleeping bag, knowing I'd have to spend the night alone on the mountain.

I realized I was still in a dangerous spot, for rocks were continually cascading down. I dragged myself behind a big rock that would be a shield for me. Soon after doing that, a huge boulder came crashing down the mountain, bounced off my shield rock, and barely grazed my sleeping bag. This rock was to me as the Lord is to me: "He is a shield to those who take refuge in him" (Prov. 30:5).

It was so steep there that several times during the night I began to slide down the mountain. I'd crawl out of the bag, pull it back up to the safety of the big rock, and try sleeping all over again.

There was no pain, which was amazing because of all the blood on me. In fact, my head would stick to the sleeping bag because of the blood that kept oozing from my face and scalp. I had to break loose from time to time so I could turn my head.

Not only was this big rock my shield, it was a shelter and symbolically I was in the protective "shadow" of the Lord. Psalm 91:1 asserts, "He who dwells in the shelter of the Most High/will rest in the shadow of the Almighty." My "dwelling place" that night was certainly in His shadow. I felt no pain or concern, because I was in the presence of the Lord. He was with me and gave me comfort.

# 24
# The Consequences

In traveling alone, I'd broken the very rule I'd given to the others. The Turkish commando was to be alongside me at all times, but I told him to go on ahead with the two who had climbed the summit.

The Greek word for the Holy Spirit is *parakletos*, meaning "called to one's side." As I had chosen to go it alone and suffered near-fatal consequences, so may we suffer spiritually if we choose to go our own way and not be guided by the Word of God through the Holy Spirit.

In John 14:16-17 Jesus says, "'And I will ask the Father, and he will give you another Counselor (Comforter) to be with you forever—the Spirit of truth. The world cannot accept him, because it neither sees him nor knows him. But you know him, for he lives with you and will be in you."

# 25
# Meanwhile ... Back at Camp

The base camp at Lake Kop and the high camp at the 14,000-foot level had walkie-talkie contact. There were predetermined check-in times.

It was Thursday evening, the day of my fall. I was lying on the mountainside, and no one knew where I was. At 6:00 PM the base camp called to check on the progress of the high-altitude search party.

The high camp reported that I'd left at mid-morning, and they wondered if I'd gotten into camp safely. The base camp naturally hadn't seen me, so the alert was out that I was missing.

It was almost dark. There would be no way they could find me in the vast wilderness of Ararat at night. It would be hard enough in the daylight!

One small group did hike after dark to the plateau area where some shepherds camped. The group asked if the shepherds had seen me. When they returned with no results, three of the people in the base camp went off alone and prayed. They linked arms and quoted Matthew 18:20, "For where two or three come together in my name, there am I with them." They prayed that I'd be found.

There was nothing to do but for everyone to go to sleep. They made plans before going to bed that the high camp would send its members down in three different routes, and that three more groups would start out in different directions from base camp. They would all select the most probable route I may have taken, but none knew about my shortcut, which was not on any of the routes they'd chosen.

# 26
# God's Nudging

In the middle of that night one of the Americans awakened in base camp at 2:00 AM. The wind was blowing at the flaps of his tent. It was bitterly cold. He was one who had linked arms and prayed earlier.

As he prayed again, he felt an indescribably strong impulse to go to a certain ridge on the north slope and look for me there. It was a place he'd been earlier in the week. He determined to find that spot with his search party the next morning. He went back to sleep until 5:00 AM.

Proverbs 3:6 admonishes, "In all thy ways acknowledge him, and he shall direct thy paths" (KJV).

# 27
# The Search Begins

Try to imagine the immensity of Mount Ararat. It is the highest mountain in Turkey at 16,945 feet and is purported to have one of the largest land masses of any single mountain in the world.

There are glaciers, canyons, snowfields, ridges, mass jumbles of broken rocks, crevices, crumbling cliffs, and streams. To find a man, especially if he is unconscious and lying in one of the tens of thousands of crevices on the mountain, would be nearly impossible.

And remember, I had not followed one of the normal routes. Instead, I had taken a shortcut across a treacherously steep snowfield.

When I awakened the next morning, I knew I was still in danger of falling rocks. I tried to move but couldn't stand up. I began pushing myself down the mountain, sliding on my backside. I knew that the sun would begin melting the snow and might dislodge more rocks. I had to reach safer ground, but in my weakened condition I didn't make it very far.

All six groups started out very early that morning—the three from the top and the three from the bottom. If they couldn't find me, one of the commandos would go down the mountain to enlist a platoon of soldiers to join the search, but they didn't want to alert the military if I had simply established a midway camp for the night.

They began walkie-talkie contact, but the Russians

must have heard of the rescue attempt, for they were on all the channels of our walkie-talkies, speaking Russian at the same time our people were talking. It made communications difficult.

This worried the searchers even more, for now they wondered if Russians, disguised as shepherds, had captured me, or if I had been taken by terrorists, or if I'd fallen down a cliff and died. The plot thickened for the searchers, but they believed they would find me. "Whatever you ask for in prayer, believe that you have received it, and it will be yours" (Mark 11:24).

# 28
# Calling My Name

Of the three groups that started out from base camp, two were comprised of two Turks each. The third group had two Turks and the one American who was going to hike toward that certain ridge where he thought he would find me.

They began the search and covered the immense mountain as well as they could. Interestingly enough, only the American called my name. As he went through the canyons, across the bottom of Parrot Glacier, and up the ridge that led to Ark Rock, he kept calling, "Jim . . . Jim . . . Jim."

This proved to be absolutely essential to my eventual rescue. He could have maintained silence as the commando and the mountaineer did. It seemed strange for him to be the only one shouting my name, but he didn't mind being different. He'd learned as a Christian to "not conform any longer to the pattern of this world" (Rom. 12:2). Finding me was more important to him than conforming to the practices of the others.

# 29
# Found!

It had been two hours since the groups started out, the ones from high camp carefully picking their way down through the ice fields and crumbling rock from the top, and the ones from base camp climbing as swiftly as they could up into the 12,000- and 13,000-foot level. It was rough going from both directions. They not only had to watch their footing on the treacherous rocks, but they were also looking for an injured or dead man.

The American from the base camp reached the base of Parrot Glacier and realized that his group was too bunched up. He sent the commando a couple of hundred yards below him to the left and the Turkish mountaineer the same distance above him to the right. They were nearing the ridge he felt directed to and wanted as much lateral visibility as possible.

When he came up onto that jagged ridge, he was right where he had envisioned it the night before. He could see far into Russia and over into Iran.

The chilly morning wind hit his face. A few minutes' pause was enough for him to hear some rocks falling from the cliffs between him and the summit. He saw nothing but the expanse of Ararat, ridge after ridge of crumbling north-slope canyons.

Once again he called my name.

I heard him!

I was no more than fifty yards away!

I answered weakly, hoping he would hear, "I'm over here, brother. I need your help." The wind was blowing from me to him, and standing on that protruding ridge, he was able to hear my soft, weakened voice. But he couldn't see me yet. I was behind some rocks.

He yelled, "Jim, I can hear you but can't see you. If you can, yell again so I can spot you."

I shouted again. Setting off a smoke signal device which alerted the other search parties, he started off toward me, though he still couldn't see exactly where I was.

I feel God answered the prayers of that small group the night before, and of the others in the expedition who had been praying, and led this search party to within fifty yards of where I was lying in a broken heap. Given the vastness of Ararat, I can think of no other answer.

James 5:16 observes, "The prayer of a righteous man is powerful and effective."

# 30
# Other Men in Danger

The bright-orange smoke alerted all the parties within sight of that part of the mountain. The ones on top appeared as dots, so it would take a long time for them to reach us.

But a search group from the high camp saw the signal, and one of the men instantly headed down a snowfield, possibly the same one that I had fallen down. He was coming to my aid. He started sliding faster and faster, so he stuck his ice axe in the snow to slow him down. It hit some rocks and flew out of his hands. Now he had nothing to brake his sliding. He began tumbling head over heels, and finally crashed into the rocks below. Badly injured, he couldn't help me; now he needed help.

Another member of one of the high camp groups saw the smoke and tried a quick descent down a cliff, but became perilously stuck on a ledge. He couldn't get up or down. Facing him was a fall of 400 feet. He had to be rescued with ropes.

My rescue was so near, but not yet a fact.

The searcher who had called my name and found me was also in trouble. There was a precipitous snowfield between him and me. The most direct route to me was for him to cross it; he didn't want to go around it. Knowing I was badly injured, he darted across the icy surface, sticking the edges of the soles of his boots into the snow and using his ice axe to support him.

After a few steps onto the snow, he was stuck. He couldn't move ahead or backward. The snow wasn't deep enough for him to get a good grip with his ice axe; it kept hitting rocks. He had a good grip with the edge of one boot, but the other one couldn't grip. The terrain was too icy. He stood precariously balanced on one foot. He couldn't lie down and pull himself across the snow because the angle was so steep—much like a church steeple slant—that he would have crashed seventy-five feet or more onto the jagged rocks below. One more step forward or backward and the same thing would have happened. He couldn't move.

He yelled to the Turkish mountaineer who had seen the smoke and was rushing to the scene. More experienced at climbing on ice, the Turk led the American to safety.

Others were willing to risk themselves for me. Jesus taught His disciples: "My command is this: Love each other as I have loved you. Greater love has no one than this, that one lay down his life for his friends" (John 15:12-13). Those men nearly did that for me.

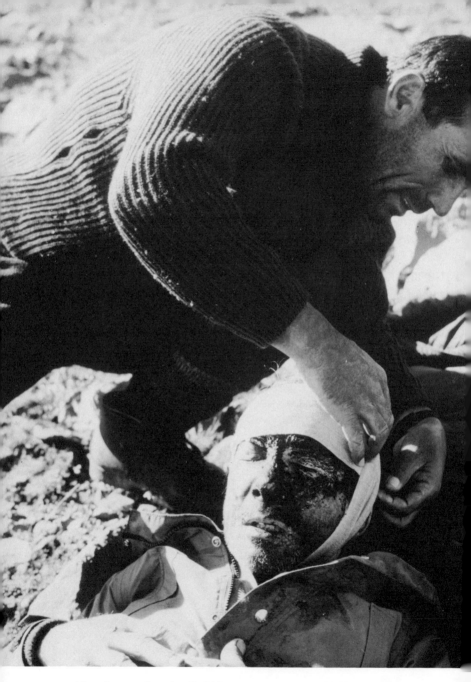

After Jim was found, a Turkish commando gave him first aid (Photo by
Monte Unger).

# 31
# The Rescue

When the Turk and the American safely traversed the ice and came toward the sound of my voice, they finally spotted me. This was around the 12,500- or 13,000-foot level, and they'd been climbing steadily for two hours. Now they were running and leaping across the sharp rocks, slipping and tripping.

They were fifteen yards from me but could simply go no further without a rest. They were totally winded. The American gasped, "Jim . . . sorry . . . got to stop . . . can't breathe." Both stood looking at me for about fifteen or twenty seconds, which seemed like an eternity to them but which was fine by me, for I had been found!

My eyes were puffy and my face was black with caked blood. It looked as if I had been burned in a fire. Flies were sticking to my face as if I were already carrion. They refused to be brushed away. The smell of sickening-sweet blood was heavy in the air. I was a mess.

They dashed the final few yards to me. The third member of that search party, the commando, joined them by this time and administered first aid from a kit he always carried with him.

To lie in the wilderness all the previous afternoon and evening, and through the cold night with the slipping and sliding, it had been such a beautiful sound to hear my name being called out in the lonely silence.

One's name is something special to a person. God also

delights in names. He named all the stars: Psalm 147:4 says, "He determines the number of the stars and calls them each by name." And in Revelation 2:17 He tells us He will give each of us "a new name," a special name known only to Him. To hear my name that day on Ararat was a special experience to me.

# 32
# The Trek to Camp

The commando and the American were going to take turns carrying me until we were down the slope to the plateau area. We didn't know it then, but it would take two hours to cover those couple of miles.

When one of them tried to lift me, my ribs and chest hurt so badly we had to try another method. They stood on either side of me; I put my arms around them (fortunately, we were all about the same height); and they carried me down the mountain, dangling me between them like a limp, rag doll. I was able to move my legs and step gingerly from rock to rock but couldn't put my full weight on my feet.

What a time it was!

None of the other groups was close enough to help, and they had to attend to their own small disasters. And we had to move from the rescue area immediately because of the falling rocks.

The mountaineer had gone back to the plateau to find a shepherd with a horse. It would have been impossible to bring the horse to where we were. We were again on those bowling-ball-type tailings that stretch down from the cliffs. There was hardly a single step of sure footing as we headed down.

After those two hours we reached the plateau. There were a number of helpers there by then. They had a stretcher and had to carry me up one more steep cliff to the plateau. From there I rode the horse for another two and a half hours back to base camp. I was safe again!

> Many, O Lord my God,
>   are the wonders you have done.
> The things you planned for us
>   no one can recount to you;
> were I to speak and tell of them,
>   they would be too many to declare
>                         (Ps. 40:5).

# 33
# How to Teach "Humanity"

At base camp I lay down on the floor of the cook tent on some thick Turkish rugs, had some cool watermelon, cold pop, and peaches. Extremely weak and dehydrated, I had to replace the fluids I'd lost. I still faced a four-hour horseback ride down the mountain to civilization.

Just as we started down, one of our guides began arguing with the shepherd who owned the horse. All of a sudden the guide grabbed a stout walking stick and whacked the shepherd on top of the head with it.

Then the guide yelled, in English, "That'll teach him humanity!"

The argument had been about money. The shepherd wanted money in advance before carrying me down the mountain. The guide asked him not to worry about payment until later, but to think of the injured man's needs first.

I was pleased the guide was looking out for me, but what an ironic way to "teach humanity." In contrast I thought of Jesus' way: "But the fruit of the Spirit is love, joy, peace, patience, kindness, goodness, faithfulness, *gentleness* and self-control" (Gal. 5:22-23, author's italics).

Jim, being led down Ararat the day he was rescued (Photo by Yucel Donmez)

# 34
# Down the Mountain

The Turkish commando officer had gone down the mountain earlier, trying to obtain a helicopter. No helicopter came, so we thought it best for us to head down and put me in the hospital.

It was not an easy trip. The shepherd with the lump on his head and the one who administered the lump took turns leading my horse. The man who had found me earlier that morning now walked beside my horse, holding my belt loop for the entire four-hour trek. He kept being knocked off the trail when it narrowed, and the horse shoved him over the edge. He'd climb back up the loose rock, grabbing my belt again to make sure I didn't fall off.

The other man who had been injured while trying to rescue me rode behind on another horse, which was led by a Turkish youth. The six of us made our way to civilization.

I hung onto the saddle horn with all of my remaining strength. The sun at the lower altitude was blazing hot. We began to see cactus. Our mouths were like cotton.

We soon forgot how cold we'd been on top; now it was just the opposite. We suffered from thirst, for we ran out of water long before we reached the bottom.

At one of the shepherds' tent villages, the Moslem women wailed and beat their arms, breasts, and legs when they saw my battered body. I must have looked pretty banged up, for my face was still caked with blood and my left eye was nearly swollen shut. And there were my broken teeth and other cuts and scratches.

We finally arrived at the highway. Though I was extremely weak, the Lord strengthened me enough to make that long, hot journey. "But the Lord is faithful, and he will strengthen and protect you" (2 Thess. 3:3).

# 35
# The Fallen Astronaut

We were fortunate to arrive at a spot on the highway where there was a small, primitive cafe. They had no soft drinks that day, only some water which we were fearful of drinking.

They did serve us some fresh tomatoes. Six Turks were sitting around us talking, staring, and gesticulating. My guide told them I'd walked on the moon. They must have thought I'd fallen from the moon from the way I looked. And now I couldn't even walk on earth!

One of them stood in the middle of the highway trying to flag down a ride to the hospital which was still a thirty-minute drive away. A car stopped.

The driver was our final angel of mercy. He drove eighty miles per hour, had one arm out the window, was looking into the backseat, and driving on the wrong side of the road much of the time. Which was safer: Ararat, with its avalanches, or this driver, filled with the excitement of the emergency drive to the hospital, weaving all over the road? We thought the ride could bring a fate worse than the fall.

When we arrived at the military hospital, which was no more than a first-aid station, the room was filled with people. There were twelve soldiers and five civilians. The doctors investigated my wounds and gave me a shot.

One of them exulted, "It's been over thirty-one hours since you bumped your head, so no need to worry about head trauma. You'll live to see more interesting things than this. You'll be OK."

A general entered the room, and the gawking soldiers evaporated.

I was eventually taken by ambulance and helicopter to a large military hospital in Ezurum, was given excellent medical care, and was able to rest for five days before going home.

The hospital commander was a plastic surgeon. This was another answer to prayer. He tended to the bad cuts on my face. There would be no ugly scars! Even in this the Lord was with me. The psalmist exclaimed:

I sought the Lord, and he answered me;
he delivered me from all my fears.
Those who look to him are radiant;
their faces are never covered with shame.
This poor man called, and the Lord heard him;
he saved him out of all his troubles (Ps. 34:4-6).

# 36
# An Ambassador for Christ

While I was in the hospital in Ezurum, I was interviewed by a Turkish radio broadcaster. This gave me a chance to tell the Turkish nation about Christ.

The announcer asked, "When you set foot on the moon you were at the summit of the materialistic and technological world. In your mission to Turkey in climbing Mount Ararat, your mission was not materialistic or technological, but a spiritual or mystical one. Now, as a person who has been in both worlds, the technological summit and the mystical summit, what are your feelings?"

I replied, "I think the satisfaction man is looking for will be in the spiritual realm rather than in the materialistic or technological area. I've seen great accomplishments in the world, yet I find people who have no inner peace within them, no personal satisfaction because they are looking in the wrong places.

"I think in order to have satisfaction one must have a personal relationship with God, because that is the most important thing. You might call it mystical. I'd call it a personal, spiritual relationship with the One Who made us and the One Who created the environment in which we live. Life takes on much more meaning when one has that personal relationship with Christ, when he knows that he is loved."

So the fall down the mountain gave me an opportuntiy to speak for Christ from my hospital bed, which is my job as an ambassador for Him.

# V.

# AFTERMATH: WHEN DOES AN ADVENTURE END?

# 37
# We Meet a Nineteenth-century Man

We'd met a Turkish commando who didn't get cold.

We also met a Turk who was a nineteenth-century man, not at all like the shepherd who wanted payment *before* his services.

He was one of the Turks who had helped with the expedition. He wasn't our official guide, but it turned out that he spoke the best English of all the Turks who accompanied us, so he became our "unofficial guide."

At our last meal in Istanbul, we wanted to give this man a generous sum of money as a token of our appreciation for his constant interpreting.

He refused to take it.

One of our men slipped the money into the man's sport-coat pocket, thinking this would work. The Turk froze and requested, "Please remove the lira from my pocket. I don't want to touch it."

Our man persisted. So did the Turk. Neither side was going to give in.

Finally, the Turk replied, "You are guests in my country. I'm not materialistic. I didn't serve you for money. I'm a nineteenth-century man."

We instantly understood his dignity and sense of honor. Our man removed the money from the Turk's pocket, and we'd learned one more truth about the people of our host country. The adventure may have been over, but our learning continued.

Proverbs 23:4 cautions: Do not wear yourself out to get rich;/have the wisdom to show restraint." There would have been nothing wrong in our eyes if this Turkish friend had taken the money. Yet, because he had "the wisdom to show restraint," our respect for him deepened considerably. He has become a noble man in our eyes.

# 38
# What the Turks Thought We Were Doing on Ararat

When we returned home, we maintained correspondence with several of the Turks.

One of them wrote, "The Turkish people really do not believe a famous astronaut would climb Agri Dagi (the Turkish name for Ararat) to find an ark. They think you were involved in putting (military) devices on the mountain."

We tend to see what is most obvious in our own grid-pattern of thinking. The Turkish people don't think much about an ark in the mountains. Instead, because they are surrounded by Syria, Russia, Iran, and Greece, they think of self-defense. So when a former astronaut-military officer climbed a mountain in an extremely sensitive zone, the Turks didn't think he is doing it for fun. They believed he was secretly working for the government.

It is unusual that we can be in earnest pursuit of one goal while others sincerely believe we are doing something totally different. So, though our ark search was the true objective, stories still buzzed throughout that ancient land that we had another mission. When we heard of their reaction, we felt like Isaiah when he cried, "Who has believed our message?" (Isa. 53:1).

# 39
# What If We Had Found the Ark?

True, it would have been a marvelous archeological find, perhaps the most important in history.

But would it have changed man or man's view of God and of the Bible? The answer is, of course, purely speculative. Many think it would be a major turning point against humanism. Others think it would have little effect.

What biblical insight do we have on this? Probably the closest lesson is the story of the rich man and Lazarus.

"The rich man also died and was buried. In hell, where he was in torment, he looked up and saw Abraham far away, with Lazarus by his side."

The rich man asked Abraham to send Lazarus "to dip the tip of his finger in water and cool my tongue." Abraham answered that such couldn't be done because of the great chasm between heaven and hell.

So the rich man pled, "Then I beg you, father, send Lazarus to my father's house, for I have five brothers. Let him warn them, so that they will not also come to this place of torment.

"Abraham replied, 'They have Moses and the Prophets; let them listen to them.'

"'No, father Abraham,' he came back, 'but if someone from the dead goes to them, they will repent.'

"He said to him, 'If they do not listen to Moses and the Prophets, they will not be convinced even if someone rises from the dead'" (Luke 16:22-31).

An expedition member appears as a tiny speck on a dark cliff of Ararat—almost in the center of the photo (Photo by Mike Carpenter).

# 40
# When Does an Adventure End?

Normally, when you complete reading an adventure book, it is all over. You will go on to other armchair adventures.

But hopefully, because of the scriptural parallels we've given, our adventure will continue to live on in you because of the living Word of God. Hebrews 4:12 states, "The word of God is living and active. Sharper than any double-edged sword, it penetrates even to dividing soul and spirit, joints and marrow; it judges the thoughts and attitudes of the heart."

It will certainly continue to burn in the hearts of those of us who went to Turkey because of the Word of God, but also because of the friends we made, the scars on our bodies, and the memory of the wind of Ararat in our faces.

I visited with the President of Turkey when I left the hospital. I was bearded, had broken teeth, and was scarred. Most of my hair was cut off; I was limping. He must have wondered who this crazy adventurer was. After I gave him a firsthand report, he invited, "Mr. Irwin, come back any time."

Some of us did return—four weeks later.

And we returned again in 1983 and 1984.

The ark will be sought year after year. It's a mystery that will live on and on until it is rediscovered. Like the smile of the *Mona Lisa*, the real answer about the ark has eluded us for centuries.

But, who knows? Maybe next year!

# About Monte Unger

Monte Unger is a free-lance writer and editor living in Colorado Springs, Colorado, where he and James B. Irwin often work together. Unger also assisted in the writing of *More Than Earthlings*, Irwin's last book with Broadman.

A native of Burlington, Iowa, Unger is a graduate of Carroll College (B.A. in history and philosophy) and has studied at Northwestern University. His posts have included: communications director for The Navigators and public relations director for the YMCA of Metro Chicago. He has been a free-lance writer since the late 1960s.

He has held membership in the Evangelical Press Association and the American Booksellers Association. He has edited a number of books for Christian publishers around the nation and has written many articles for Christian journals and magazines.

He and his wife, Linda, have three sons, Erik, Brent, and Brandon. The family hobbies are hiking, backpacking, jogging, collecting stamps, tennis, travel, reading, and collecting exotica.